THE ENCOURAGING THE HEART WORKBOOK

revised edition

JAMES M. KOUZES BARRY Z. POSNER

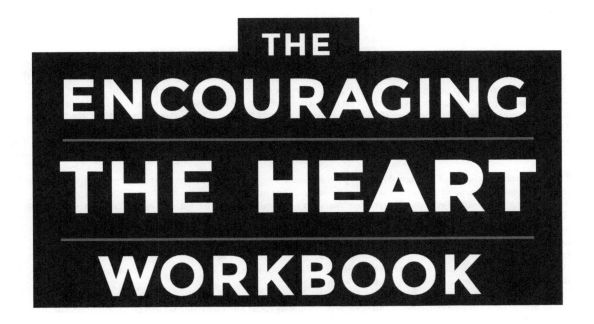

THE
ENCOURAGING
THE HEART
WORKBOOK

revised edition

Published by The Leadership Challenge®
A Wiley Brand
One Montgomery Street, Suite 1200, San Francisco, CA 94104-4594
www.leadershipchallenge.com

For additional copies or bulk purchases of this book or to learn more about The Leadership Challenge®, please contact us toll free at 1-866-888-5159 or by email at leadership@wiley.com.

For more information about Wiley products, visit www.wiley.com..

ISBN: 978-0-470-87683-1

Acquiring Editor: Lisa Shannon
Director of Development: Kathleen Dolan Davies
Production Editor: Dawn Kilgore
Editor: Rebecca Taff
Manufacturing Supervisor: Becky Morgan

Printed in the United States of America

Printing   10   9   8   7   6   5   4

Contents

Introduction

*If you don't show your appreciation to your people, then they're going to stop
caring, and then you're going to find yourself out of business.*

—LuAnn Sullivan, Wells Fargo Bank

THE HEART OF THE MATTER

At the heart of leadership is caring. Leadership is a relationship between those who aspire to lead and those who choose to follow. Sometimes the relationship is one-to-many. Sometimes it's one-to-one. But regardless of whether the number is one or one thousand, leadership is a relationship. And as a relationship, leadership requires a connection between leaders and their constituents over matters, in the simplest sense, of the heart.

We need heart because the struggle to the top is arduous. If we're going to make it to the summit, we need someone shouting in our ear, "Come on, you can do it. I know you can do it!" We need applause. We need to know that we're connecting to others in order to do our best. We need to feel connected to others and, in turn, they to us, because greatness is never achieved alone.

When leaders commend individuals for achieving the values or goals of the organization, they give them courage, inspiring them to experience their own ability to deliver—even when the pressure is on. When we recognize people for their contributions, we expand their awareness of their value to the organization and to their co-workers, imparting a sense of connectedness that, being social animals, all humans seek.

Encouraging the Heart, then, is about the principles and practices that support our basic human need to be appreciated for who we are and what we do. It's about how leaders can apply these principles and practices to their daily work.

LEADERSHIP IS EVERYONE'S BUSINESS

The Encouraging the Heart Workbook and its companion, *The Encouragement Index*, have their origins in more than twenty-five years of research on the practices of individuals when they were functioning at their personal best as leaders.

After collecting thousands of best-practice leadership case studies and analyzing tens of thousands of leadership assessment instruments, we've come to the conclusion that leadership is not a place, it's not a position, and it's not a secret code that can't be deciphered by ordinary people. The secret of high-performing organizations is that everyone within them knows that leadership at all levels is expected and rewarded, and that individuals everywhere are responsible for making extraordinary things happen.

The Five Practices of Exemplary Leadership®

Encouraging the Heart is one of the five leadership competencies that our research shows are essential to getting extraordinary things done in organizations. When leaders are at their personal best, they:

Model the Way. Leaders clarify values by finding their voice and affirming shared ideals, and they set the example by aligning actions with shared values.

Inspire a Shared Vision. Leaders envision the future by imagining exciting and ennobling possibilities, and they enlist others in a common vision by appealing to shared aspirations.

Challenge the Process. Leaders search for opportunities by seizing the initiative and by looking outward for innovative ways to improve. They also experiment and take risks by constantly generating small wins and learning from experience.

Enable Others to Act. Leaders foster collaboration by building trust and facilitating relationships. They strengthen others by increasing self-determination and developing competence.

Encourage the Heart. Leaders recognize contributions by showing appreciation for individual excellence. They also celebrate values and victories by creating a spirit of community.

All of The Five Practices are essential to exemplary leadership. All contribute to explaining why leaders are successful. In this workbook, you will focus on the fifth practice, Encouraging the Heart. If you'd like to know more about the others, they are explained in detail in our book, *The Leadership Challenge.*

WHO SHOULD USE THIS WORKBOOK?

This workbook is designed for anyone in any type of leadership role. Its purpose is to help you further your abilities to lead others to get extraordinary things done. Whether you're in the public or private sector, an employee or volunteer, on the front lines or in the senior ranks, a student, a teacher, or a parent, this workbook will help you develop your capacity to guide others to places they've never been before. There are two main ways to use the workbook: (1) in a self-study program for leaders desiring to develop their skills and abilities for Encouraging the Heart and (2) in a facilitated group learning session designed to give leaders an idea of their strengths and opportunities for improvement in the practice of Encourage the Heart.

WHAT'S INCLUDED

Here's an overview of what's in the workbook:

Chapter 1: How to Use This Workbook. An overview of how to use the workbook for self-study and in a facilitated learning setting descriptions of the activities; and guidelines and suggestions for completing the workbook.

Chapter 2: The Seven Essentials of Encouraging the Heart. An introduction to the seven essentials of Encouraging the Heart that will help you become a caring and credible leader.

Chapters 3—9: Mastering the Essentials. Information and activities to help you master each of the seven essentials.

Chapter 10: Moving Forward. Using what you learned by developing an action plan.

OBJECTIVES

When you complete *The Encouraging the Heart Workbook,* you will be able to:

- Explain why the practice of Encourage the Heart is the "heart of leadership"

- Describe the seven essentials of Encourage the Heart

- Describe several ways for implementing each essential in your own role as a leader

- Develop an action plan for improving your ability to Encourage the Heart

BEFORE YOU BEGIN

Although this workbook includes what you need to understand the Encouraging the Heart essentials and apply them in your own role as a leader, we recommend that you begin your development by reading our book, *Encouraging the Heart*. The stories and examples in the book will give you a fuller understanding of the ways in which mastering this practice helps leaders become more successful at achieving extraordinary results.

We also recommend that you take a look at *The Leadership Challenge,* which explains our research into leaders' best practices, describes The Five Practices of Exemplary Leadership® Model, and provides stories of leaders who exemplify each of the practices. You'll find more information on our website, www.leadershipchallenge.com.

Best wishes as you begin your journey into becoming a better leader. Keep in mind that you make a difference.

James M. Kouzes
Orinda, California
Barry Z. Posner
Santa Clara, California

Chapter 1

How to Use This Workbook

Encouraging the Heart *is about the basic human need to be appreciated for who we are and what we do.*

—Jim Kouzes and Barry Posner

The best leaders see every one of their experiences as a learning opportunity. But there's a catch. Unexamined experiences don't produce the rich insights that come from reflection and analysis. Thus, if you want to become a better leader, you need to study your own behavior and become more conscious about the choices you are making and how you act on your intentions. That's what the activities in this workbook will help you do. There are two main ways to use the workbook: (1) on your own, in a self-study program to assess and develop your skills and abilities to Encourage the Heart, and (2) in a facilitated group learning session where you will gain an idea of your strengths in the practice of Encourage the Heart and identify opportunities for improvement.

LEARN, REFLECT, APPLY, ASSESS

Whether you are working on your own or participating in a group learning session, the *Encouraging the Heart Workbook* gives you information, questions, and activities that are designed to help you in the learning process.

- The *reflection questions* will help you think about what you learn. We've provided these questions to challenge your thinking and to help you become more conscious about how well you engage in the behaviors related to each of the seven essentials of Encourage the Heart.

- The *activities* will help you apply what you learn to your role as a leader. We've included lots of activities because we believe that one important way people learn is through experience.

- The *assessment questions* will help you evaluate the results of the activities—the results of applying what you're learning about the seven essentials.

GUIDELINES FOR COMPLETING *THE ETH WORKBOOK*

Following an ETH Workshop

Selected learning activities plus reflection and assessment questions will be on the workshop agenda, and the facilitator will direct you to the appropriate pages in this workbook for working through them. After attending an Encouraging the Heart (ETH) workshop, we recommend you work through the rest of the workbook on your own to enhance your understanding and solidify your skills. In doing so, you can follow the guidance below for working on your own, except that you will not repeat activities or questions already covered in your workshop.

Working on Your Own

If you haven't had the opportunity to learn about how to Encourage the Heart in a workshop or other group learning session, you can use the workbook to develop your leadership skills on your own.

After you finish reading the Introduction and this chapter, work through Chapter 2, which provides the foundation for understanding the seven essentials of Encouraging the Heart.

Although we suggest following the order of the workbook, you can, if you wish, complete Chapters 3 through 9 in any order. For example, you might prefer to start with the essentials on which you most need to work.

Save Chapter 10 for last. In that chapter, you'll pull together everything you've learned and develop an action plan for moving forward.

Whether or not you go through the chapters in order, do the following to make sure that you get the full benefits of the work you do:

- *Schedule the time.* We're all so busy these days that we seldom get things done unless we schedule the necessary time to do them. Treat completing this workbook the way you'd treat any important project—write it into your calendar.

  The ETH Workbook is not designed to be completed at one sitting. Many of the activities ask you to apply what you learn over a period of time and then return to some questions about your experiences and observations. We recommend that you allow yourself four weeks to complete the entire workbook.

- *Answer all the questions and do all the activities.* The questions and activities in this workbook are designed to help you learn. If you think you already know the answer to a question, already have a good understanding of a concept or topic, or are already skilled in a behavior, pause long enough to make sure before moving on to the next part of the workbook.

The Seven Essentials of Encouraging the Heart

Everybody wants to feel that they matter. You can get a lot accomplished by making other people feel important.

—Manish Chandra, Siebel Systems

DOES ENCOURAGEMENT MATTER?

In a survey we conducted, we asked people: "Do you need encouragement to perform at your best?"

How would you respond?   _____ Yes   _____ No

What percentage of the survey respondents would you estimate said "Yes" to this question?

_____ 1 to 20 percent

_____ 21 to 40 percent

_____ 41 to 60 percent

_____ 61 to 80 percent

_____ 81 to 100 percent

Here's another question we asked: "When you get encouragement, does it help you perform at a higher level?"

How would you respond?   _____ Yes   _____ No

What percentage of the respondents would you estimate said "Yes" to this question?

_____ 1 to 20 percent

_____ 21 to 40 percent

_____ 41 to 60 percent

_____ 61 to 80 percent

_____ 81 to 100 percent

What We Found

When we asked, "Do you need encouragement to perform at your best?" we were surprised that only about 60 percent of the respondents answered, "Yes." It turned out that many people believed that they didn't _need_ encouragement—that they _could_ do their best without it.

Yet we knew from our research that people performed at higher levels when leaders gave them encouragement. So we re-framed the question. When we asked, "When you get encouragement, does it help you perform at a higher level?" about 98 percent said yes. These responses are in line with a study by the training and development company Kepner-Tregoe, in which researchers found that 96 percent of the North American workers they studied agreed with the statement, "I get a lot of satisfaction out of knowing I've done a good job."[1]

THE RECOGNITION SCORECARD

How much recognition do you think that American workers report typically receiving?

_____ % never get recognized.

_____ % receive little recognition for a job well done.

What percentage of managers do you think report giving recognition for high performance?

_____ % giving recognition.

What We Found

Researchers report that about one-third of North American workers say they NEVER are recognized for a job well done. Slightly more (44 percent) report that they receive little recognition for a job well done. Only 50 percent of managers say they give recognition for high performance.

Considering the fact that encouragement and recognition lead to higher performance, why do you think those percentages are so low?

_____

_____

_____

_____

_____

Below are three reasons why people do not receive and managers do not give more encouragement. You might also have come up with some other reasons.

- Managers assume that outstanding performance is just part of the job

- The stereotype that "professionals" or "adults" don't need any recognition as an integral part of their motivation and drive to be successful

- Expressing genuine appreciation for the efforts and successes of others means we have to talk about our feelings in public, making ourselves vulnerable to others

A SECRET REVEALED

For years, we've operated under the myth that leaders ought to be cool, aloof, and analytical; they ought to separate emotion from work. We're told that real leaders don't need love, affection, and friendship. "It's not a popularity contest" is a phrase we've all heard often: "I don't care if people like me. I just want them to respect me."

Nonsense.

Tony Codianni, director of the Training and Dealer Development Group for Toshiba America Information Systems, told us that "Encouraging the Heart is the most important leadership practice, because it's the most personal." Tony believes leadership is all about people, and if you're going to lead people you have to care about them.

The Center for Creative Leadership in Colorado Springs has studied the process of executive selection, and their results support Tony's observation.[2]

Of the following three factors from the FIRO-B*—an assessment developed by Will Schutz to measure interpersonal relationships—which one do you think distinguished the highest-performing from the lowest-performing managers, according to their research?

The three factors:

———— Inclusion

———— Control

———— Affection

The Center for Creative Leadership found that the single factor that differentiated the top from the bottom was higher scores on affection. Contrary to the myth of the cold-hearted boss who cares little about people's feelings, the highest-performing managers show more warmth and fondness toward others than do the bottom 25 percent. They get closer to people, and they're significantly more open in sharing thoughts and feelings than their lower-performing counterparts.

In other words, the best leaders want to be liked, and they want openness from other people. Not caring how others feel and think about what we do and say is an attitude for losers (and very self-centered and aloof or out-of-touch individuals)—an attitude that can only lead to less and less effectiveness. The evidence tells us that expressing affection is important to

*The FIRO-B measures two dimensions of three factors: the extent to which a person both expresses and wants (1) inclusion, (2) control, and (3) affection. See W. Schutz, *The Human Element: Productivity, Self-Esteem, and the Bottom Line*. San Francisco: Jossey-Bass, 1994.

success, and we all need it. In fact, too many people have a secret they're afraid to reveal because it might make them look soft or wimpy. We all really do want to be loved.

When we interviewed former chief executive officer and current venture capitalist Irwin Federman, his remarks foreshadowed what we now know from the data. He spoke an important truth about the *chemistry* that exists between great leaders and those who follow them. He spoke of love as a necessary ingredient, one that is rarely appreciated, in part because we underrate the role of our feelings:

> You don't love someone because of who they are; you love them because of the way they make you feel. This axiom applies equally in a company setting. It may seem inappropriate to use words such as love and affection in relation to business. Conventional wisdom has it that management is not a popularity contest. . . . I contend, however, that all things being equal, we will work harder and more effectively for people we like. And we will like them in direct proportion to how they make us feel.[3]

When we wrote our book, *Encouraging the Heart,* we asked people to identify the most important non-financial reward they could receive at work. What response do you think they gave?

You might be surprised to learn that the most common answer was, "A simple thank-you."

Author Gerald H. Graham reports that personal congratulations rank at the top of the most powerful non-financial motivators identified by employees.[4] Harvard Business School Professor Rosabeth Moss Kanter reports that in the most innovative companies there is a significantly higher volume of thank-you's than in companies of low innovation.[5]

As you go through this workbook, keep in mind the basic message of this chapter: At the heart of effective leadership is genuinely caring for people.

MY MOST MEMORABLE RECOGNITION

Think back over the times when someone has personally recognized and rewarded you for outstanding performance—the times when someone showed you genuine appreciation for what you accomplished. Select one time that you would consider your most memorable recognition—a time when you felt the most appreciated by another person.

What made that recognition so memorable? What did the other person do to recognize you? What actions did he or she take? Recall the story in as much vivid detail as you can.

Describe the situation: What was your accomplishment?

_____

_____

_____

_____

_____

Describe the setting: Where did this recognition take place?

_____

_____

_____

_____

_____

Describe the other person's actions: What did the person do and say? Be as specific as you can.

_____

_____

_____

_____

_____

Describe the effect on you: How did the recognition make you feel?

_____

_____

_____

_____

_____

Draw some conclusions: Based on your experience, what makes recognition truly meaningful and enduring? What are the implications for you, as a leader?

_____

_____

_____

_____

_____

_____

THE SEVEN ESSENTIALS OF ENCOURAGING THE HEART*

While he was president of North American Tool and Die (NATD), Tom Melohn enjoyed giving out monthly "Super Person" Awards, which the company presented to employees who went the extra mile to help it move toward its goal of the highest-quality products. Over the years we've used Tom as our best-practices example of how a leader can Encourage the Heart.

There's one situation, in particular, that truly exemplifies all the essential principles and actions that form the foundation of this practice. Read the story of the Super Person Award ceremony that follows. Pay particular attention to the way Tom interacts with Kelly and "the gang," as Tom affectionately calls them, that has gathered to witness the award. Notice what he does and how the group responds.

Tom Melohn's Super Person of the Month Celebration

Shop employees are gathered in the NATD's employee break area, near the boxes and machinery of the plant, for a Super Person of the Month Award ceremony.

"We've got a new award today," Tom announces to the assembled group. "It's called the North American Tool and Die 'Freezer' Award. Now, who knows what that's for and who won it? Anybody got an idea?"

Somebody shouts out: "Kelly!"

"There's something in the freezer," Tom says. "Kelly . . . go on, Kelly, look in the freezer. Come on. Hurry up!"

Kelly opens the door of a nearby freezer and reaches inside. He finds a metal rod and cylinder with an envelope stuck to them.

Tom laughs. "Come on up here."

Everyone joins in the joy and laughter as Kelly walks up and Tom shakes his hand. Tom laughs some more, obviously delighted with the fun the group is having at this ceremony. Tom takes the envelope and metal rod out of Kelly's hand.

"Oh, that's cold!" Tom exclaims. He hands the envelope back to Kelly and sets the metal part on a table.

Kelly opens the envelope and pulls out a check for fifty dollars.

"Okay?" Tom asks Kelly.

"Yeah!" Kelly says, smiling shyly.

*If you are familiar with the latest editions of *The Leadership Challenge* or *The Leadership Challenge Workshop*, you will notice a discrepancy in the number of essentials associated with Encouraging the Heart. This workshop is designed to offer participants a deeper, more extensive discussion of this Practice, hence the presence of more essentials in this undistilled experience.

"Remember this job?" Tom asks the group. "I went through the shop one day and I saw Kelly going into the freezer. I thought, 'What the hell is going on? Is he goofing off or making margaritas, or what?' You know what he did? He couldn't get this [*Tom points to the metal rod*] into here [*he points to the metal cylinder*], so he said, 'Hey, I'm going to put this in the freezer. It'll shrink, and then I'll put the part together.' And it worked!

"And I said, 'Where'd you get that idea?'

"And he said, 'What? It's just part of the job, right?' " Tom looks at Kelly.

"Yep," Kelly says.

Tom turns to Kelly, puts his arm around his shoulder, and says, "What else can I say, gang? God love you, baby. God love you." Then he turns to the group, holds the part in the air, and says, with pride and caring in his voice: "And remember: no rejects, no rejects, no rejects! That's why we're here, gang."**

Take a few moments to think about that story.

What precisely did Tom do? What actions did he take?

_____

_____

_____

_____

_____

What words did he use? What nonverbal behaviors did he exhibit?

_____

_____

_____

_____

**If you'd like to watch this scene and an in-depth interview with Tom about leadership and employee partnership, they're in the film *In Search of Excellence: The Video*, available from Video Arts, www.videoarts.com. Tom has also written a book that describes his philosophy and experience at NATD. T. Malohn, *The New Partnership: Profit by Bringing Out the Best in Your People, Customers, and Yourself*. Essex Junction, VT: Oliver Wright, 1990.

What values did he exemplify that encouraged the heart?

_____

_____

_____

_____

_____

Here are some of the typical responses to this story; yours might be different.

- Tom was genuine; he was a real person.

- He saw Kelly do this; he was out on the shop floor, and he took note of it.

- He showed that he believed in people.

- He put his arm around Kelly.

- He really loved his employees.

- He made it fun.

- He recognized Kelly in public, not behind a closed door in his office.

- He told a story about what Kelly did.

- He didn't just talk about recognition, he lived it.

- He gave out the award himself; he didn't delegate it.

- He was clear about the standards: total quality.

- He repeated the statement "no rejects" several times.

- He gave Kelly a check, sharing some of the organization's benefit from Kelly's action.

- He laughed and had a good time. He really enjoyed recognizing Kelly and being with the employees.

A close analysis of this "Freezer Award" ceremony—and others like it—teaches us that underlying the practice of Encouraging the Heart is a set of recognizable, learnable, and repeatable actions that leaders take to make people feel special and to reinforce the standards of the enterprise. We call those actions "The Seven Essentials of Encouraging the Heart."

THE SEVEN ESSENTIALS

When leaders do their best to Encourage the Heart they:

1. Set Clear Standards

2. Expect the Best

3. Pay Attention

4. Personalize Recognition

5. Tell the Story

6. Celebrate Together

7. Set the Example

1. Set Clear Standards

At the close of the Super Person of the Month ceremony, Tom said, "Remember: no rejects, no rejects, no rejects! That's why we're here, gang."

Tom had a clear set of standards that he expected people in the organization to live up to. The most important for NATD was no rejects!

In recognizing individuals, we sometimes get lost in the ceremonial aspects. Recognitions are reminders; quite literally, the word "recognize" comes from the Latin to "know again."

Recognitions are opportunities to say, "I'd like to remind you of what's important around here. Let me give you one example of how someone in this organization demonstrated what it means to meet or exceed our standards."

The first prerequisite to Encouraging the Heart is to set clear standards. In this entertaining moment, Tom linked the reward with the standards that had been set. The reward was for an action in service of a clear purpose.

To be successful in Encouraging the Heart, it's critical that everyone cherish a common set of standards. (We've chosen to use the word standards to mean goals, expectations, or objectives as well as values or principles.) By clearly defining the values and expectations for which we're held accountable and by linking performance to those standards, leaders establish a benchmark for achievement.

However, not just any standards will do. They must be standards of excellence. They must be aspirational, bringing out the best in us. Certainly, "no rejects" is a lot more aspirational and inspirational than, say, "Five out of ten will do." By repeating the standard, Tom reinforces a crucial principle for employees of North American Tool and Die. He links appropriate performance to the reward, signaling that if someone follows this model of behavior, other rewards follow.

2. Expect the Best

It's clear from the story that Tom cares, and that he really believes that the people on the front line can achieve a standard of no rejects. Tom puts it this way: "In my judgment, the best leaders have two characteristics: an unswerving, single-minded, utterly all-consuming set of values and a belief in the innate goodness of human beings. All the energies of the best leaders are dedicated to helping people achieve their full potential."[6]

Tom is right. The best leaders believe people can achieve the high standards that have been set. It's called the Pygmalion effect: Even if others don't believe in themselves initially, the leader's belief becomes a "self-fulfilling prophecy."

Belief in others' abilities is fundamental to Encouraging the Heart. We give off certain cues that say, "You can do it, I know you can do it." Passionately believing in people and expecting the best of them is another prerequisite to Encouraging the Heart.

3. Pay Attention

"I went through the shop one day . . ." Tom told us. He's a wanderer, a leader who walks around, who is right there with you. He's a leader in the truest sense of the word—a venturer who delights in "catching people doing things right."

But it's more than just walking around. It's also paying attention and understanding the significance of people's actions. You've probably heard of "MBWA," managing by walking around. Tom calls it "CBWA": *caring* by walking around.

Tom didn't just notice that Kelly was doing something unusual. He engaged him in conversation. When he realized what Kelly was actually doing, Tom understood that his actions were the very embodiment of the standards NATD wanted people to maintain.

Leaders are always on the lookout for exemplars of the organization's values and standards. Wherever they are, whatever they're doing, the best leaders have a special radar that picks up positive signals.

4. Personalize Recognition

Although the Super Person of the Month recognition was a regular feature at NATD, Tom customized the award and the ceremony just for Kelly. He gave it a unique, attention-getting name: the North American Tool and Die *Freezer Award,* tying it specifically to something that Kelly—and nobody else—had done. He made it even more meaningful by putting the metal part in the freezer so that when the time came Kelly would go back to the freezer, open it, and take out the part, illustrating what he had done in the first place. This was clearly not something that happened every day. The fact that it was unusual, fun, and dramatic all helped to imprint the event and the stated values in people's minds.

This emphasis on the individual uplifted Kelly and sent the message to others that singular efforts really can make a difference.

Before recognizing someone, then, the best leaders get to know people personally. They learn about their likes and dislikes, their needs and interests. Then, when it comes time to recognize a particular person, they know a way to make it special, meaningful, and memorable.

5. Tell the Story

Why tell the story? Why not just give Kelly the check and public recognition and then have him sit down? Why take the time to re-enact what was done?

Let's see how the ceremony might have gone without the story.

"We've got another Super Person Award today," Tom announces. "Let's see, who won it? Let's think. Oh, yes, Kelly. Kelly won it. Come on up here, Kelly."

Everyone watches passively as Kelly walks up to the front of the room. Tom hands Kelly the monthly Super Person plaque and a check for fifty dollars.

"Thank you, Kelly," Tom says matter-of-factly. "You really showed us what it means to implement our policy of zero defects."

"Remember," he continues, turning emotionlessly to the group, "no rejects, no rejects, no rejects. That's why we're here, everyone."

Not only would that ceremony be boring, but everyone, including Kelly, would forget about it the instant it was over. It would not be memorable in any way.

Throughout history, storytelling has been used to convey the values and ideals shared by a community. In fact, research tells us that stories have more of an impact on whether people believe information than does straight data. The story is just as crucial to Encouraging the Heart.

Stories are not only to entertain, they're to teach. Good stories move us, and they cause us to remember. By telling the story in detail, Tom illustrated what everyone, not just Kelly, could do to live by the standard of no rejects. He not only told the story, he had Kelly re-enact a portion of it. Told in that way, stories capture our attention, exciting and entertaining us. At the same time, the narration of what happened provides a behavioral map that we can easily store in our minds.

Stories also enable us to see ourselves. We learn best from those we can most relate to— people most like ourselves.

Although the live example is the most powerful, you can use stories in newsletters, annual reports, advertisements, even on voice mail and in e-mail, to Encourage the Heart and teach positive lessons about what people do to exemplify our values. That's sure a lot more powerful than posting a list of our values on a wall.

6. Celebrate Together

Imagine for a moment that Tom did call Kelly into his office to give him the award privately. The scene might go something like this:

"Kelly, I heard that you did something to help us achieve our goal of no rejects. To thank you for your initiative, here's a check for fifty dollars."

"Thanks," says Kelly.

They shake hands. As Kelly walks out the door, Tom stops him and says, "One more thing. Please don't tell anyone else you got this. It might not be clear to them what happened and might cause some friction on the floor, and we don't want that."

In that scenario, Kelly would have an extra fifty bucks in his pocket, but he couldn't tell anyone. He couldn't be proud of what he'd done. He couldn't receive congratulations. Tom achieved far more by recognizing Kelly in public. There was no point in simply telling the story in private; Kelly already knows what he did. The story was for the benefit of others. Stories are how groups learn lessons. The public ceremony provides a setting for broadcasting the message to a wider audience.

Many of us are reluctant to recognize people in public situations, perhaps fearing that it might cause jealousy or resentment. But if the leader is genuine, that doesn't happen. Most of us want others to know about our achievements, and the public ceremony does that, sparing us the need to brag about ourselves. Leaders who recognize others publicly know from experience that public recognition rarely causes hard feelings.

Today's leaders are discovering that Encouraging the Heart through public events builds trust and strengthens relationships. By lifting people's spirits in this way, we heighten awareness of organizational expectations and humanize the organization's values and standards, motivating people at a deep and enduring level. Even more, public recognition serves as a valuable educational mechanism, demonstrating company values and encouraging others to duplicate the actions that they see rewarded.

Public ceremonies also bring people closer together. As we move to a more virtual world, where so much of our communication is by voice mail, e-mail, cell phone, videoconferences, and pager, it's harder for people to find opportunities to be together. Social support is absolutely essential to our well-being and to our productivity. Celebrating together is one way we can get this essential support.

7. Set the Example

You can't delegate Encouraging the Heart. Every leader must take the initiative to recognize individual contributions, celebrate team accomplishments, and create an atmosphere of confidence and support. "Do unto others as you would have them do unto you" clearly applies here. Leaders set the example for others. They practice what they preach. If you want others to Encourage the Heart, begin by modeling it yourself. You can't expect others in the organization to follow your lead if you don't take the first step yourself.

That's certainly what Tom did. He set high standards. He believed in others. He invested his attention in them. He personalized the recognition. He told the story. He celebrated with others. He set the example.

Personal involvement also demonstrates a genuine expression of caring. It helps foster trust and partnership. Leadership is a relationship, and relationships are formed only when people come into contact with each other.

Tom also put his money where his mouth was in other ways. He made the recognition tangible by presenting Kelly with a check for fifty dollars and putting Kelly's name on a plaque that went on public display. When combined with all the rest, these tangible rewards helped memorialize the event. The money confirmed that the organization took the action seriously. The plaque reminded everyone that the organization appreciates people who demonstrate the behaviors consistent with the values and standards.

IT'S NOT EASY TO ENCOURAGE THE HEART

Supporting others, particularly in times of great change, can be physically and emotionally draining. We have learned that Encouraging the Heart is one of the most difficult of The Five Practices of Exemplary Leadership®. We've found that it's much easier for leaders to Challenge the Process, for example, than it is for them to Encourage the Heart.

But the seven essentials of Encouraging the Heart are core leadership skills. They are not just about showing people they can win for the sake of making them feel good. When striving to raise quality, recover from disaster, start up a new service, or make dramatic change of any kind, leaders must make sure that people experience in their hearts that what they do matters.

Chapter 3

Set Clear Standards

People get energized when they know what values and behaviors are required to achieve the goal.

—Hongwei Zhou, KLA-Tencor

At the close of the Super Person of the Month ceremony, Tom Melohn said something that is crucial to understanding how to be most effective in Encouraging the Heart. He said, "Remember: No rejects, no rejects, no rejects! That's why we're here, gang."

The first prerequisite, then, to Encouraging the Heart is to set clear standards. The standards were as much the subject of the NATD Freezer Award as was the action that won Kelly his reward. In this entertaining moment, Tom linked the reward with the standards that had been set.

As we pointed out earlier, by *standards* we mean both goals and values (or principles). Both have to do with what's expected of us, although goals connote something shorter-term, whereas values and principles imply something more enduring. Typically, values and principles serve as the basis for goals; they define the arena in which goals must be set.

The challenge for us as leaders is to make sure that *everyone* understands the standards, and that *everyone* takes every possible opportunity to recognize others for contributing to achieving high standards.

GOALS PLUS FEEDBACK KEEP US ENGAGED

Researchers studied soldiers who underwent several weeks of arduous training, during which they were competing for places in special units. At the end of their training, one final challenge remained: a forced march in full gear.[7]

The soldiers were divided into four groups. Each group would march twenty kilometers (about twelve and a half miles) over exactly the same terrain on the same day.

Below are the instructions that each group received. Which group do you think performed the best and experienced the least amount of stress? On the blank lines, rank the groups from 1 to 4: 1 = best performance, least stress; 4 = worst performance, most stress.

_____ Group 1: Told the exact distance they would march—20 kilometers—and regularly informed of their progress along the way.

_____ Group 2: Told only, "This is the long march you've heard about." Nobody knew exactly how far they would march, nor were they informed of their progress along the way.

_____ Group 3: Initially told they would march for fifteen kilometers. After marching fourteen kilometers, they were told they had six more to go.

_____ Group 4: Told they would march twenty-five kilometers. After marching fourteen, they were told they had six more to go.

The researchers found that Group 1 performed the best and had the least amount of stress. Knowing how far they were going and getting regular reports were the keys to achieving the highest ratings.

Group 2 performed the worst and had the most stress. Knowing only that "this is the long march you've been waiting for," not knowing how far they were to march, and receiving no information along the way yielded poor results.

Group 3 received the second-highest rating, and Group 4 finished third. But in both instances, the results were much closer to Group 2 than to Group 1.

People need to know whether they're making progress or just marking time. Goals serve that function, but it's not enough simply to know that we want to make it to the summit. We need to know whether we're still climbing, or if we're sliding downhill.

Stanford University's Albert Bandura found that people's motivation to increase productivity on a task increases only when they have a challenging goal and receive feedback on their progress.[8] But goals without feedback, and feedback without goals, have little effect on motivation. People ask, "Zero rejects? Why are you giving me feedback about that? I didn't know that was our goal!" Clear goals and detailed feedback help people become self-correcting, more easily understanding their place in the big picture, and determining what help they need from others and who might benefit from their assistance. Under these conditions, they're willing to put forth more productive effort.

Think about this for yourself: How important is having clear goals and helpful feedback when you're engaged in a challenging task? What difference do they make to your motivation?

_____

_____

_____

_____

One form of feedback is encouragement. Encouragement tells us we're making progress, on the right track, and living up to the standards. But the wonderful thing about encouragement is that it's more personal than other forms of feedback. To be encouraging requires us to get close to people, show that we care about them, and demonstrate that we are interested in others. Encouraging the Heart strengthens trust between leaders and constituents, a relationship that is absolutely critical to getting extraordinary things done in organizations.

Encouraging the Heart also speaks *to* people's hearts—to deeply held values and beliefs, to something beyond the material—and contributes to creating meaning in the workplace. When leaders unequivocally communicate clear standards, they honor everyone's desire to do their very best. They elevate the human spirit.

REFLECT ON SETTING CLEAR STANDARDS

- What values and principles do you most cherish?

_____

_____

_____

- How do you communicate these beliefs to others?

_____

_____

_____

- How clear are you and how clear are your constituents about the goals they are expected to achieve and the standards they are expected to meet?

_____

_____

_____

- To what extent is the feedback you give your constituents clearly tied to the standards that have been set?

_____

_____

_____

- How do you, and how do your constituents, know success when it happens? How do you and they see it, experience it, feel it?

_____

_____

_____

- How are you getting feedback on how you're doing as a leader?

_____

_____

_____

ACTIVITIES FOR SETTING CLEAR STANDARDS

Below are some activities that can help you learn more about setting clear standards and apply what you've learned in the chapter.

- Think of someone you admire who exemplifies living a principle-centered life. Interview that person. Find out how that person discovered his or her own values. Note the key points of what you learned below.

_____

_____

_____

_____

_____

_____

- Meet with your team members or colleagues to discuss the organization's values. Ask everyone to share what those values mean to them. Listen and observe. What common perspectives does everyone seem to share? What perspectives seem to be unique to some individuals? Are there any major values conflicts? Discuss how you can honor individual perspectives and also have common values that govern your collective behavior as a team. Summarize the results of the discussion.

_____

_____

_____

_____

_____

_____

- The next time someone on your team begins a project, clarify the standards. Then give the person feedback to let him or her know how well the standards were achieved. Note the results below.

_____

_____

_____

_____

_____

_____

Chapter 4

Expect the Best

Set the bar high and people will surpass your expectations.
—Dewey "Buddy" Blanton III, Rockwell Collins Display Systems

In playwright George Bernard Shaw's play, *Pygmalion,* which became the well-known musical *My Fair Lady,* Professor Henry Higgins, a teacher of phonetics, transforms a Cockney flower girl named Eliza Doolittle into a lady. Because Professor Higgins believes so strongly that Eliza can learn to speak and act like a lady, she does more than that: She actually becomes one.

The best leaders believe that, no matter what their role, people can achieve the high standards that have been set. It's called the Pygmalion effect. It's a belief so strong that even if others don't believe in themselves initially, the leader's belief—or the teacher's or the parent's or the colleague's—gives rise to self-confidence, to a belief of "Yes, I *can* do it."

Belief in others' abilities is fundamental to the practice of Encouraging the Heart. Like it or not, our beliefs about people are broadcast in ways we're not even aware of. We give off cues that say to people either "You can do it, I know you can do it" or "There's no way you'll ever be able to do that: Why bother trying?"

After all, how can you expect someone to get extraordinary things done if he or she picks up the signal that you don't believe he or she can? And even if you said, "Thanks, great job," how genuine would it be perceived to be?

Most of us have experienced this phenomenon at one time or another. Think of a time when someone let you know that he or she really believed you could do something. What did that person say? What did that person do? What was the effect on you?

_____

_____

_____

_____

_____

Think of a time when someone let you know that he or she thought you would fail at something. What did that person do? Say? What was the effect on you?

_____

_____

_____

_____

_____

Leaders communicate expectations in a number of ways. Leaders with positive expectations establish a climate that makes people feel more at ease. They offer positive reinforcement; they give others the information, opportunity for input, and resources necessary to do their jobs; and they are likely to lend assistance and give out better assignments.

It's common sense that higher expectations would result in better performance, right? So no manager in her right mind would think or act differently, right?

Not true. Professor Jean-François Manzoni and research fellow Jean-Louis Barsoux at INSEAD, in Fontainebleau, France, found that "Bosses—albeit accidentally and usually with the best intentions—are often complicit in an employee's lack of success. How? By creating and reinforcing a dynamic that essentially sets up perceived under-performers to fail. . . ."[9]

In a reversal of the great-expectations dynamic of the Pygmalion effect, the set-up-to-fail syndrome can begin quite innocently. An apparent performance problem or personal conflict between an employee and his or her manager triggers an increase in the manager's supervision and control. The employee begins to believe that the manager lacks trust and confidence in him or her. Eventually, these real or perceived low expectations cause the direct report to stop making independent decisions or taking initiative, which reinforces the manager's original assessment that the individual is a poor performer. Thus, the problem intensifies.

Can you think of a time that you created a dynamic that set up someone to fail? Describe the situation and the results. If not, how did you keep from falling into this common trap?

_____

_____

_____

_____

_____

Our own research shows that people are often anxious or nervous when they are encouraged by people in leadership positions to deliver their personal best. But in our surveys of people who experienced such challenges, when leaders held high expectations for them, they marched in and did what was expected without hesitation. Spurred on by their leaders' high expectations, they developed self-confidence that gave them the courage and volition to live up to their leaders' expectations.

What's your opinion about whether the people you lead can learn the skills required to do their jobs? Can they acquire them, or are they mostly innate?

_____

_____

_____

_____

_____

Our beliefs can't be weighed and measured like the raw materials that come in and the finished products that run off the assembly line. But seen or not, measurable or not, they have an enormous impact on the people around us. Exemplary leaders know this and know how to purposefully hold in their minds high expectations for themselves and other people.

REFLECT ON EXPECT THE BEST

Think of several people you lead. How would you honestly rate your expectations of those people? Write their names or initials on the lines below, then check the appropriate boxes.

		Level of Expectation	
	High	Moderate	Low
Person #1 _____	☐	☐	☐
Person #2 _____	☐	☐	☐
Person #3 _____	☐	☐	☐
Person #4 _____	☐	☐	☐
Person #5 _____	☐	☐	☐

Think about one or two of the lowest-level performers among those you lead. Briefly describe the ways in which your expectations might be influencing their performance.

Performer #1

_____

_____

_____

_____

_____

Performer #2

_____

_____

_____

_____

_____

Think about one or two of the highest-level performers among those you lead. Briefly describe the ways in which your expectations might be influencing their performance.

Performer #1

_____

_____

_____

_____

_____

Performer #2

_____

_____

_____

_____

What are some positive changes you can make immediately in the way you demonstrate your expectations of these people you've identified and all other people you lead?

_____

_____

_____

_____

ACTIVITIES FOR EXPECT THE BEST

Below are some activities that can help you learn more about expecting the best and apply what you've learned in the chapter.

- Put a "Smile" sign on the console of your car. (Seriously, try it.) Every day when you drive to work, practice smiling. Try it for a week. Note the results below.

_____

_____

_____

_____

_____

- The next time you talk to one of your constituents about a difficulty he or she is having with a project, make sure that some time during the conversation you say, "I know you can do it," or words to that effect. Note the results below.

_____

_____

_____

_____

_____

- Are the messages conveyed in your organization mostly positive or mostly negative? Walk around and examine the images on the walls. Listen to the way people talk to one another. Analyze the organization's written communications. Note your observations below. What might be changed?

_____

_____

_____

_____

_____

- For the next two weeks, look for opportunities to communicate positive messages to the people you work with: "That's a great idea"; "You really did a good job with that project"; "I appreciated what you said in the meeting"; and so on. Note the results below.

_____

_____

_____

_____

_____

_____

_____

_____

_____

_____

_____

_____

_____

_____

Chapter 5

Pay Attention

What makes a difference is being able to understand what other people are feeling.
No one likes being ignored.

—Manish Mathuria, Arsin Corporation

Leaders are out and about all the time. They're attending meetings, visiting customers, touring the plants or service centers, dropping in on the lab, making presentations at association gatherings, recruiting at local universities, holding roundtable discussions, speaking to analysts, or just dropping by employees' cubicles to say hello. None of these wanderings should be purposeless. Leadership is not a stroll in the park; leaders are out there for a reason. One of the reasons, we maintain, is to show that they care.

How did Tom Melohn know that Kelly had come up with a great new idea? "I was walking through the plant one day," he said. That gives us an immediate clue as to the kind of leader Tom is. He's a wanderer, a walk-arounder, a leader who is right there with you. He's a leader in the truest sense of the word—a venturer. We quickly learn from the scenario at NATD that Tom is a leader who delights in "catching people doing things right."

But it's more than just catching people doing things right. It's also paying attention and understanding the significance of their actions. If you are clear about the standards of behavior you're looking for, and if you believe and expect that people will perform like winners, then you'll notice lots of examples of people doing things right and doing the right things.

Do you lead by "wandering around"? List some examples of things you've noticed recently whereby people are meeting or exceeding the expectations that have been set:

_____

_____

_____

_____

Look at your list. Would you say you notice more positive or more negative things?

_____

_____

_____

_____

What do you think are the consequences of a leader noticing that people are doing things right?

_____

_____

_____

_____

What do you think are the consequences of a leader looking for what people are doing wrong?

_____

_____

_____

_____

It's only human nature that if we feel we're being watched by someone who is looking for our faults, we act very differently than we do in a supportive environment in which we know there's an opportunity to be rewarded for special achievement. If we know someone is looking for positive examples, we make an effort to reveal them.

If people know there's a caring leader in their midst, patrolling the organization in search of achievements to celebrate, they relax and try to offer the best of themselves. This positive focus on behavior and performance, linked to goals and values, significantly improves morale as it moves the company toward higher levels of performance and increased productivity.

In a supportive climate, people will also be much more likely to help each other succeed. They will teach and coach each other—another boost to productivity. In addition, people will be more likely to let you know when problems are brewing and lend a hand in solving them before they escalate.

Think of a time when a leader created a supportive, encouraging climate for you and your colleagues. What did the leader do and say? What were the results?

_____

_____

_____

_____

_____

Now think of a time when a leader seemed to be on the lookout for people who were doing things wrong. What did that leader do and say? What were the results?

_____

_____

_____

_____

Paying attention demands that you put others first. Empirical studies demonstrate that the best leaders put others at the center of the universe.[10] Looking out for number one is not what effective leaders believe and practice.

Central to putting others first is the capacity to walk in their shoes. Learning to understand and see things from another person's perspective is absolutely crucial to building trusting relations and to career success.[11] To understand another person's perspective requires listening, a crucial leadership skill, but not just any kind of listening.

One of our colleagues tells a poignant story that illustrates what real listening is. A young girl whose best friend couldn't speak and couldn't hear learned sign language so she could communicate with her friend. "Now," the girl said, "I listen with my eyes and my heart, not just my ears and my brain."

Think of a time that someone really listened to you. What did the person do? What did he or she say? What was the effect on you?

_____

_____

_____

_____

How well do you listen? Do you listen carefully enough to learn what other people are thinking and what they're feeling? Rate yourself on this scale:

I Listen Very Poorly   **I Listen Very Carefully**

1   2   3   4   5   6   7

What do you do to give people opportunities to be listened to?

_____

_____

_____

_____

_____

Eyes-and-heart listening can't be from a distance, from reading reports or hearing things second-hand. Our constituents want to know who we are, how we feel, and whether we really care. You have to get physically close to people if you're going to communicate. This means regularly walking the hallways and plant floors; meeting often with small groups; and hitting the road for frequent visits with associates, key suppliers, and customers. It may even mean learning another language if a large portion of your workforce or customer base speak it.

But managerial myth says we can't get too close to our associates—we can't be friends with people at work. What do you think?

_____

_____

_____

_____

_____

Well, you can set that myth aside. In a study conducted over a five-year period, professors Karen Jehn of the University of Pennsylvania's Wharton School and Pri Pradhan Shah of the Carlson School of Management at the University of Minnesota discovered that groups of friends performed far better on motor-skill and decision-making tasks than groups of people who knew each other only slightly (with the proviso that the friends are strongly committed to the group's goals).[12]

People are just more willing to follow someone they like and trust. To become fully trusted, we must be open—to others, but also *with* others. This means disclosing things about yourself—talking openly about your hopes and dreams, your family and friends, your interests and your pursuits. Once a leader takes the risk of being open, others are more likely to take a similar risk—and thereby take the first steps necessary to build interpersonal trust.

Asking for constructive feedback is another way to be open. When you're out there paying attention to the positive contributions people are making, stop and ask them for feedback. It's a demonstration that you appreciate them. "How am I doing?" is a practice of the best leaders. Recognizing another's contribution is your gift to others. Feedback is their gift to you. It's a gift of information that enables you to grow and improve.

When you really pay attention—when you're curious, when you look for the best, when you put others first, when you listen with eyes and heart, when you hang out, when you open up to and with others—then you find what you're seeking. You notice all kinds of examples of people living up to and exceeding the standards that have been set. You find lots of opportunities to recognize individuals for their contributions.

REFLECT ON PAYING ATTENTION

- How well are you doing in leading by walking around? In noticing what your constituents are doing right? How do you think you might become a more attentive leader?

_____

_____

_____

_____

_____

- How open are you with your constituents? What have you told them about your hopes, dreams, joys, passions, life? What do you know about their hopes and dreams? How many of your colleagues would introduce you as their "friend"?

_____

_____

_____

_____

- Do you ask your constituents for feedback? How often? How do you ask them? Do you find their feedback helpful? Is there something you need to change about your approach?

_____

_____

_____

_____

- Can you think of a constituent who currently exemplifies the organization's standards? When was the last time you let that person know how you felt?

_____

_____

_____

_____

- Have you ever noticed the credits that come after a movie? The producers recognize virtually everyone who took part. Can you do that with everyone who works on the "movie" you're making right now? Pretend that you're making a movie and write out a list of "credits" that captures everyone's contributions:

_____

_____

_____

_____

_____

_____

ACTIVITIES FOR PAYING ATTENTION

Below are some activities that can help you learn more about paying attention and apply what you've learned in the chapter.

- During the next two weeks, leave your work area for fifteen minutes every day for the sole purpose of "caring by wandering around." As soon as you return to your work area, record your observations in a notebook or in a computer file. Pay attention to the following:

  Things that people are doing right. Record the people's names. Describe the setting and the people involved. Note the ways in which the act is special and how it fits with the standards you're trying to reinforce. Be as specific as you can. Later, you'll use this information to develop your recognition stories.

  Your colleagues and constituents. Talk with people to learn more about them. What are their needs and aspirations? What do they need to find greater joy in their work? How do they like to be rewarded?

- When the two weeks are up, use the space below to summarize the key points of what you learned from caring by wandering around.

_____

_____

_____

_____

_____

- Start a Recognition Ideas file on your computer or in a notebook that you carry with you. Record ideas for recognizing and rewarding individual contributions and for celebrating team accomplishments. When you pay attention, you'll find that ideas are all around you—at work, at home, on television, in books. After two weeks, write the three best ideas below.

_____

_____

_____

_____

_____

- Practice paying attention. Your ability to attend to the most common and immediate elements of your daily life helps you be more attuned to what is going on around you. Set aside twenty to thirty minutes when you won't be disturbed. If you'd like, you can do this activity at home or outdoors. Focusing on one thing at a time, notice everything you can about the following:

    Your breathing. Pay attention to how your breath moves in and out of your body. What happens when you breathe in? What happens when you let a breath out?

    What you hear. Close your eyes and pay attention to what you hear. What sounds are reaching your ears? Are they loud or soft? Harsh or pleasant? Do they trigger images in your mind? If people are speaking, can you distinguish words? Notice everything you can about the sounds you hear.

    What you feel. Still with your eyes closed, notice the way the air feels on your face and the clothes feel on your body. Is the air warm or cold? Wet or dry? Still or moving? Are your clothes tight or loose? Rough or soft?

    What you smell and taste. Also with your eyes closed, become aware of any odors. Do you smell perfume? Gasoline? Flowers? Food? Cleaning supplies? Is there a taste in your mouth? What is it?

    What you see. Opening your eyes, notice what first comes into your line of vision. Be aware of colors, lines, and textures. Slowly turn your head to the right, then to the left. Up and then down. Pay attention to everything you see.

- When the time is up, write down everything you noticed:

_____

_____

_____

_____

Chapter 6

Personalize Recognition

I spend lots of time getting to know everyone on the team so that I can figure out what each person needs to feel appreciated and valued.

— Walt Shaw, Juniper Networks

Remember what Tom Melohn did to make the Super Person of the Month Award special for Kelly? He gave it a unique, attention-getting name: The North American Tool and Die *Freezer Award,* tying it specifically to something that Kelly and no one else had done. Tom personalized the award and customized the ceremony just for Kelly. By doing that, he made the award more meaningful and memorable, not only for Kelly, but for his co-workers.

One of our colleagues, Steve Farber, is an extremely accomplished trainer and presenter who gets a lot of thank-you notes. But one of the notes he received was very special. The note was sent to Steve, but it was addressed to Steve's son. The person who sent the note, Carl English, vice president of electric transmission and distribution at Consumers Energy in Jackson, Michigan, could have purchased a preprinted thank-you card and written a perfunctory note inside about how much he enjoyed being in Steve's class. But Carl had paid attention. He'd learned that Steve had a son who was curious about what his dad did at work. So he wrote the note to the son, praising his dad for an exemplary job.

That extra little effort made the note something that Steve treasures and loves to share with others. Says Steve, "It made a huge difference. . . . On those days when I'd rather be at home than out on the road somewhere, I think of that note, and it reminds me of why I go to work every day."

Has anyone ever given you an award or recognized you in some other way that was particularly meaningful and memorable to you? What did the person say and do to make the award meaningful and memorable?

_____

_____

_____

_____

_____

Have you ever received an award or recognition that you did not find especially meaningful or memorable? While you might have been pleased to receive it, what was lacking?

_____

_____

_____

_____

_____

Before recognizing someone, the best leaders get to know people personally. They observe them in their own settings. Then when it comes time to recognize a particular person, they know a way to make it special, more meaningful, and more memorable.

To truly recognize people, you have to know something about them—what interests them and what doesn't, what they like and dislike, whether they enjoy public recognition or shirk from it, and even what they are or are not willing to take credit for. Otherwise, the act of recognition might have little or no meaning—and it could even cause discomfort. For example, someone who is not interested in sports is unlikely to appreciate tickets to a basketball game as thanks for a job well done. And a shy person who dislikes public attention might be embarrassed by being called onstage to receive an award.

A leader who's out there scouting regularly can learn a person's likes and dislikes from friends, co-workers, family members, and direct observation. Most of the time, it should not be necessary to ask the recipient directly; but when in doubt, what's wrong with asking?

Think of a time when you showed your appreciation to someone or when you honored someone for his or her accomplishments. What did you do and say? Do you think the person found the recognition meaningful and memorable? If so, why? If not, why not?

_____

_____

_____

_____

_____

Ann Cessaris of Key Communication reminds us all of another reason why it's essential to personalize, or even "culturalize," recognition. "I had a client," she reported, "who was born in Asia, came to this country at age twelve, and was very well acclimated to life in the United States. However, when his boss rewarded his exceptional contribution to a team project by giving him a delightful corner office, he was horrified. He felt it destroyed the feeling of teamwork and his future relations with his team members.

"Cultural values run deep," says Ann, and she's absolutely correct. Personalizing is about knowing someone so well that you know what's appropriate for the person both individually and culturally.

Has anyone ever given you a gift or a recognition that made you feel that the person understood what you liked and appreciated? One that disappointed you or that you felt was inappropriate? Describe how it felt in each instance.

_____

_____

_____

_____

_____

What it comes down to is thoughtfulness: the effort you put into thinking about what would make the recognition special for a particular individual. It's asking: "What would really make this special and unique for this person—make it a memorable, one-of-a-kind experience? What could I do to make sure that she never forgets how much she means to us? What can I do to make sure he always remembers how important his contributions are?"

REFLECT ON PERSONALIZE RECOGNITION

- Thinking about your own experiences giving and receiving recognition, what does it take to make recognition truly meaningful and enduring?

_____

_____

_____

_____

_____

- How many of your most meaningful recognitions involved large sums of money or expensive gifts, etc.? What conclusion do you draw from this finding?

_____

_____

_____

_____

_____

- Have you ever received a letter or note of recognition that you have kept for a long time? Why did you keep it?

_____

_____

_____

_____

_____

- Do you regularly write thank-you notes when your constituents do something especially considerate or helpful or something that exemplifies the organization's standards? What can you do to make sure the notes you write are meaningful and memorable?

_____

_____

_____

_____

_____

- How many cultures are represented among your workforce? How aware are you of how each of these cultures expresses appreciation and responds to recognition? What can you do to learn more?

_____

_____

_____

_____

_____

- What do you know about what would honor each of your key constituents? List the names of five of them below. What would honor each of them?

_____

_____

_____

_____

_____

- What steps can you take to learn more about what kinds of recognition each of your constituents would find meaningful and memorable?

_____

_____

_____

_____

_____

ACTIVITIES TO PERSONALIZE RECOGNITION

Below are some activities that can help you to learn more about personalizing recognition and to apply what you've learned in this chapter.

- Ask several friends or colleagues to tell you stories about times in their lives when they received recognition that particularly moved or affected them. Ask why they found the recognition memorable and meaningful. Write down several ideas that come out of those talks.

\
\
\
\
\

- In a notebook or a computer file, make a list of all your constituents. Note what you now know about the kinds of rewards and recognition each person would appreciate and find meaningful and those that the person would not be likely to appreciate. Continue to add ideas so that you are ready when it comes time to recognize someone for an achievement.

- Plan a recognition for one of your constituents. Ask yourself, "What can I do to make sure this is special, dramatic, and unique for this person? How can I do the equivalent of addressing a letter to the person's son?" Describe the recognition below. Afterward, note the results.

\
\
\
\
\

Chapter 7

Tell the Story

In the end it's all about the story that gives people meaning to not only what we're doing but to what we're aspiring to achieve.

—Fred Hoar, Miller/Shandwick

Storytelling is one of the oldest ways in the world to convey values and ideals shared by a community. Before the written word, stories were the means for passing along the important lessons of life. We know how important they are in teaching children, but sometimes we forget how important they are to adults.

The story is just as crucial to Encourage the Heart. But why tell the story? Why take the time to re-enact what had been done? What difference does it make?

Stories are not meant only to entertain. They're also intended to teach. Good stories move us. They touch us, they teach us, and they cause us to remember. They enable the listener to put the behavior in a real context and to understand what has to be done in that context in order to live up to expectations.

Take this example from research. Stanford University organizational sociologists Joanne Martin and Melanie Powers studied the impact of stories on MBA students, an often numbers-driven, highly competitive, skeptical audience. Martin and Powers compared the persuasiveness of four methods of convincing the students that a particular company truly practiced a policy of avoiding layoffs.[13] In one situation they used only a story to persuade people. In the second, they presented statistical data that showed that the company had significantly less involuntary turnover that its competitors. In the third, they used the statistics *and* the story, and in the fourth, they used a straightforward policy statement made by an executive of the company.

Which method do you think was *most* believable to the MBA students? Which was *least* believable? (Use a check mark for your choice.)

	Most Believable	Least Believable
1. Story only	_____	_____
2. Statistics only	_____	_____
3. Statistics and story	_____	_____
4. Policy statement	_____	_____

As you probably anticipated, the most believable was number 1, the story only. The students who were given only the story believed the claim about the policy more than any of the other groups and remembered it better several months later. The executive delivering the policy statement was the least convincing.

Research clearly demonstrates that information is more quickly and accurately remembered when it is first presented in the form of an example or story.[14] Researchers have found, for instance, that when American history textbooks were translated into the story-based style of *Time* and *Newsweek,* students were able to recall up to three times more information than they were after reading a more typical school text.[15]

Howard Gardner, the Harvard professor of education who has done extensive research on the development of human intelligence, argues that "the artful creation and articulation of stories constitutes a fundamental part of the leader's vocation. Stories speak to both parts of the human mind—to reason and to emotion. And I suggest, further, that it is *stories of identity—* narratives that help individuals think about and feel who they are, where they come from, and where they are headed—that constitute the single most powerful weapon in the leader's literary arsenal."[16]

Stories put a human face on success. They tell us that someone just like us can make it happen. They create organizational role models that everyone can relate to. Stories make standards come alive. They move us and touch us. By telling a story in detail, leaders illustrate what everyone needs to do to live by the organizational standards. They communicate the specific and proper actions that need to be taken to resolve tough choices. They bring people together around the campfire to learn and have fun.

Can you think of a story someone told that helped you learn? What did you learn? What did the storyteller do to make the story come alive?

_____

_____

_____

_____

_____

When was the last time you told a public story about someone who did something extraordinary in your organization?

_____

_____

_____

But what makes a good story? According to scientist and researcher Gary Klein, a good story is a blend of several ingredients.[17] Here are the ones he sees in the stories he collects:

- *Agents:* the people who figure in the story

- *Predicament:* the problem the agents are trying to solve

- *Intentions:* what the agents plan to do

- *Actions:* what the agents do to achieve their intentions

- *Objects:* the tools the agents use

- *Causality:* the effects (both intended and unintended) of carrying out the actions

- *Context:* the many details surrounding the agents and actions

- *Surprises:* the unexpected things that happen in the story

Think about the story Tom Mehlon told in terms of those ingredients:

Agent:

_____

Predicament:

_____

_____

Intentions:

_____

Actions:

_____

_____

Objects:

_____

_____

Causality:

_____

Context:

_____

_____

Surprises:

_____

_____

Here are the ingredients you might have noticed:

Agent: Kelly.

Predicament: Kelly is faced with the problem of figuring out what to do with two components that won't fit together. He's also faced with the prospect of rejecting a part in a "no-reject" culture. If he throws away the part, he is not living up to the NATD standards. From Tom's telling of the story, you can almost get inside Kelly's head. You can imagine Kelly saying to himself, "If I throw these components out, then it will mean that they'll be scrap. That violates our standard of 'no rejects.' What can I do so that I don't waste them?"

Intentions: It's clear from the story that Kelly intended to get the rod and cylinder to fit together and make sure he lived up to the standard of no rejects. Kelly told Tom (and Tom told the NATD employees) that he had come up with the inventive idea of putting the metal rod in the freezer to see if it would shrink.

Actions: Kelly tried out his idea. He put the rod in the freezer.

Objects: A freezer and two metal components, a rod and a cylinder.

Causality: "It worked." The effect of the action was that the rod and cylinder fit together, and the no-rejects standard was maintained.

Context: The recognition took place in the setting in which the incident occurred—right there on the plant floor. Tom even managed to bring the actual freezer into the story. Not only did Tom tell the story, but he re-enacted it. It was more than a story; it was almost a play.

Surprises: Putting the metal rod in the freezer was an unexpected action. Additionally, Tom's re-enactment during the ceremony itself was full of surprises.

REFLECT ON TELL THE STORY

- How comfortable are you at telling public stories? What, if anything, is getting in your way?

_____

_____

_____

_____

_____

- What are the stories that are told most often in your organization? What are the lessons, the morals, that are being communicated? Are these the lessons that should be communicated? What other stories should be told?

_____

_____

_____

_____

_____

- Who's the best storyteller you know personally? How can you find ways to learn from this person?

_____

_____

_____

_____

_____

ACTIVITIES FOR TELL THE STORY

Below are some activities that can help you learn more about telling the story and apply what you've learned in the chapter.

- • During the next two weeks, hold a team meeting for which the only agenda item is telling stories on the theme of "I heard something good about you." Note the results below:

_____

_____

_____

_____

_____

- • Think of the best movie you ever saw that tells a compelling story. Rent it during the next two weeks and watch it again. What lessons did you learn about storytelling? How can you incorporate those lessons into your leadership practice?

_____

_____

_____

_____

_____

- Use the guide below to construct a story to convey someone's success. When you're done, practice telling the story to a colleague. Then tell the story at a team meeting or a special event. A good story only takes three to five minutes to tell. What's important is to authentically communicate the contributions that someone made.

  1. **Identify the actor(s).** Who is the person (or the people) you want to recognize. Name names. If you're recognizing a group or a team, name every member. Don't just say "the folks in accounting" or "the national account managers."

  _____

  _____

  _____

  _____

  2. **State the predicament.** What problem was solved? What standard was at stake? Don't pass up the chance to remind people of the values and principles that were involved. It's one thing to praise people for solving a problem, but it's more powerful to also praise them for living up to the organization's beliefs.

  _____

  _____

  _____

  _____

  _____

  _____

3. **Clarify the actor's intentions.** What went through the person's mind as she weighed her options? What were the members of the group thinking about? To answer this question, you'll have to talk to the actor(s) about the incident. This goes back to the essential of paying attention. To tell a good story, you need to pay attention.

_____

_____

_____

_____

_____

_____

4. **Paint—or re-enact—the scene.** What was the context? Where and when did this incident occur? Describe the surrounding circumstances. Set the stage; paint the scene. If you can actually take people to the place where it occurred, the way Tom Mehlon did, all the better.

_____

_____

_____

_____

_____

_____

_____

5. **Describe the actions.** What did everyone involved do and say? Relate in as much detail as you can what happened. Can you re-enact the process? It's important to describe the behaviors because the next time others are faced with a similar predicament they can recall "what Kelly did." They have a model of the kind of action they ought to take. The actions that they do take may not be precisely those that someone else did, but at least they'll have a framework for action. If possible, include objects (props), the way that Tom included the metal rod and cylinder. Objects help a story come alive.

_____

_____

_____

_____

_____

_____

6. **Tell how it ended.** What's the punch line? What happened as a result of the actions? Never leave your audience hanging. Tell them what happened in the end and why it was important.

_____

_____

_____

_____

_____

_____

7. **Include a surprise.** What made this incident unique? Interesting? Memorable? Funny? Every great story includes some kind of surprise. If possible, find a way to add an element of amazement. A surprise adds interest, makes the story more memorable, and produces more fun. It might even get a laugh.

_____

_____

_____

_____

_____

_____

_____

_____

_____

_____

_____

_____

_____

Chapter 8

Celebrate Together

Getting everyone together to celebrate was key. People knew that I had noticed what they contributed and how we were all in this together.

—Mark Taylor, Symantec

Can you remember the last time you celebrated something with a group in your organization or workplace? What was the reason for the celebration? What did you and your colleagues do to celebrate? What did the celebration accomplish?

_____

_____

_____

_____

_____

Celebrations—whether to recognize the accomplishment of one person or to cheer the achievements of many—are opportunities for leaders to build healthier groups. Highly visible public recognition builds self-esteem. It also builds a sense of community and belonging, of working together to achieve shared goals and shared victories.

Celebrations—public statements by their very nature—give expression to and reinforce commitment to key values. They visibly demonstrate that the organization is serious about adhering to its principles. When planning a celebration, every leader should ask, "What meaning am I trying to create?" When individuals or teams are singled out for recognition in a public event, they are held up as role models. Public recognition offers leaders the chance to convey the message, "Here's someone just like you. You can do this!"

Think back to the way in which Tom Melohn recognized Kelly. He didn't just call Kelly into his office and thank him for a job well done. He used the occasion for a celebration. Tom knew that far more is achieved by recognizing people in public. Kelly already knew what he had done. Tom told the story for the benefit of others. Public celebrations are how groups learn lessons and how we demonstrate that we are not alone in trying to accomplish great things.

Many of us are reluctant to recognize people in public situations, perhaps fearing that it might cause jealousy or resentment. But this concern is far too exaggerated, and it stands in the way of enhancing performance.

Most people want others to know about their achievements and the public ceremony does that, sparing them the need to brag about themselves. The experience of leaders who recognize others publicly is that it rarely causes hard feelings, and in most cases it helps to bring people closer.

Can you think of a time that you did something well and wanted others to know about it? Did you tell other people about your accomplishments? If not, why not? Did someone else do the "bragging" for you? If so, how did that feel?

_____

_____

_____

_____

_____

Public ceremonies serve another powerful purpose. They bring people closer together. As we move to a more virtual world where communication is by voice mail, e-mail, cell phone, videoconferencing, and pager, it's becoming more and more difficult for people to find opportunities to be together. We are social animals, and we need to know that we are connected with one another.

Those who are fortunate enough to have lots of social support, as compared to those who have little, are healthier human beings. Social support is essential to our well-being and to our productivity. Celebrating together is one way we can get that essential support.

Our need for affiliation is what motivates us to celebrate. We want other people to share in our lives, and we want to share in theirs. People need people; otherwise we'd all be hermits.

Here's a little experiment you can try to find out how true this is: Take a tour of your facility. Notice what people have sitting on their desks, stuck to their bulletin boards, or hung on the walls. As soon as you return, write down what you've seen.

_____

_____

_____

_____

_____

You probably saw lots of framed photos of people's friends and family. Awards and diplomas. Paintings and posters. Trophies and tributes. What do these things signify? Why do people put all these things on public display?

_____

_____

_____

_____

_____

We put things on public display to remind ourselves of what we've accomplished, of places we've been, of people we love. We also put our mementos on display because we want to involve others in our lives. The photos, posters, and plaques are all ways of inviting people to join us in our experience.

What do you have on display in your own office or work area? What do those things mean to you? Why do you put them on public display?

_____

_____

_____

_____

_____

_____

The things you put on display say, "Here's something important to me. Here's something that gives me joy and meaning. Ask me about it." If we didn't want others to share in these experiences, we'd keep them hidden and secret. What is public is meant to be shared.

People come together for celebrations, ceremonies, and rituals for lots of different reasons. Organization development consultant Cathy DeForest provides these examples:[18]

- *Organizational change and transition:* expansions, reorganizations, closings, mergers, the end of an old technology and the introduction of a new one, moves to new locations

- *Success:* financial success, promotions, awards, expansions to new markets

- *Loss:* of old procedures, financial opportunities, contracts, a job, status, a colleague who has just died, an experiment that ended in failure

- *People:* team successes, founders, winners of sales contests, employee awards, individual birthdays, marriages, reunions, doing good deeds for others

- *Events:* a company's anniversary, opening day, holidays, articulation of an organization's vision

Reviewing that list, what reason can you find to call people together during the next week?

_____

_____

_____

_____

_____

REFLECT ON CELEBRATE TOGETHER

- What kinds of celebrations do you hold to recognize people's accomplishments? How often do you hold them? What reasons do you use as opportunities for celebrations?

_____

_____

_____

_____

_____

- How frequently do you celebrate accomplishments? Is it often enough?

_____

_____

_____

_____

- How much socializing is going on in your organization? Are people getting enough opportunity to get to know each other? To build networks of support? Should you be doing anything differently?

_____

_____

_____

_____

_____

_____

- How have you used celebrations to create role models for others?

_____

_____

_____

_____

_____

_____

_____

ACTIVITIES FOR CELEBRATE TOGETHER

Below are some activities that can help you learn more about celebrating together and apply what you've learned in the chapter.

- Think of a reason for bringing people together within the next two weeks to celebrate the accomplishments of one person or the group. Visit a party store in your area and pick up some things to make the celebration festive. Describe the results.

_____

_____

_____

_____

_____

_____

- End your next team meeting with a round of public praise for everyone on the team. Describe the results.

_____

_____

_____

_____

_____

_____

- Visit an organization that you know has a reputation for being a fun place to work. Sit in on some of their celebrations or interview some of the people to learn about how they celebrate together. Summarize what you learned.

_____

_____

_____

_____

_____

_____

- Put a microwave near your office door. Every afternoon about 3:00, make some popcorn. Invite people to take a break and join you for a brief discussion about how the day is going. (As an alternative to popcorn, how about an ice cream vending machine or a basket of fruit?) After two weeks, note the results.

_____

_____

_____

_____

_____

_____

Chapter 9

Set the Example

The saying that talk is cheap definitely applies when you're trying to lead others. It is the example that I set that people really notice and respond to.

—Jennifer Golden, Fresh Express

You can't delegate the practice of Encouraging the Heart. Every leader—every person, in fact—in the organization has to take the initiative to recognize individual contributions, celebrate team accomplishments, and create an atmosphere of confidence and support. It's not something we should wait around for others to do. "Do unto others as you would have them do unto you" clearly applies here.

The foundation of leadership is credibility. Think about a leader you know personally whom you admire and respect. It can be someone you know now or someone you used to know. Write that person's name here:

_____

Now think about what the word credible means to you. Why do you say that the person is "credible"?

_____

_____

_____

_____

Chances are, you think the leader is credible because she can be counted on to do what she says. Over and over again people tell us credibility is "doing what you say you will do"— DWYSYWD for short. Leaders *set the example* for others. They practice what they preach. If you want others to Encourage the Heart, start by modeling it yourself.

Above all, people want to believe in their leaders. They want to believe that a leader's word can be trusted, that he will do what he says. Our findings are so consistent over such a long period of time that we've come to refer to this as the first law of leadership: If you don't believe in the messenger, you won't believe the message.

We all know about organizations that have a reputation for excellent customer service and for being fun places to work—for being cultures of celebration and recognition. Those organizations attract and retain employees and customers far better than their competitors. People form a strong bond with these institutions and are proud to be affiliated. They enjoy being a part of the experience. How do you think these organizations earn such a reputation?

_____

_____

_____

_____

_____

The most consistent answer we hear is, "Our leaders model it." Bill Miller, corporate director of employee development and senior vice president of The Money Store, put it this way: "From the heart emanates from the top." Over and over again, it's the same story. Wherever you find a strong culture built around strong values—whether they are about superior quality, innovation, customer service, distinctiveness in design, respect for others, or just plain fun—you also find endless examples of leaders who personally live the values.

Can you think of a leader in your organization (or in another organization) who sets the example by personally living the organization's values? Describe some ways in which the leader does that:

_____

_____

_____

_____

_____

If you want to create and sustain a culture of celebration and recognition, you've got to set the example. Your actions send signals about who you are and about what you expect of others. If your constituents are able to see and hear you thanking people for their contributions, telling stories about their accomplishments, and taking part in celebrating successes, then chances are that you will see them doing the same. You also have more credibility when you ask others to Encourage the Heart. They're more likely to believe you're serious about it. To excel as a leader, you must come to terms with the fact that people believe what you do, not what you say.

Setting the example for Encouraging the Heart starts, in fact, by giving yourself permission to do so. It starts with putting it in your daily planner . . . When you talk to everyone about it . . . When you turn a routine task into something fun . . . When you give to others first . . . When you get personally involved. When leaders become personally involved in Encouraging the Heart, the results are always the same: The receiver and the giver both feel uplifted. The reflection in the mirror is the one you portray.

REFLECT ON SET THE EXAMPLE

- What's one thing that you've done in the last week to Encourage the Heart at work?

_____

_____

_____

_____

- What else have you consciously done recently to send a signal to people that Encouraging the Heart is important to you?

_____

_____

_____

_____

- What would happen if you made Encouraging the Heart a part of your daily life? What would be the first thing that you'd do or would do more of ?

_____

_____

_____

_____

- How personally involved are you in the recognition and celebrations that now go on in your organization?

_____

_____

_____

_____

- What are some special ways in which you can demonstrate your appreciation of others in your workplace?

_____

_____

_____

_____

- Think about the most credible person in your workplace. What does that person do that makes you think of him or her as credible? How can you incorporate these attributes into your habits?

_____

_____

_____

_____

ACTIVITIES TO SET THE EXAMPLE

Below are some activities that can help you learn more about setting the example and apply what you've learned in the chapter.

- Use the worksheet on page 84 to do a DWYSYWD audit. In the left-hand column, record your values—the principles by which you say you want to lead your organization. In the right-hand column, record your actions—what you do on a regular basis to live out each of your values. Be completely honest with yourself. If you don't see yourself doing anything to live out a value, leave the space blank. If you think your behaviors are contrary to your espoused values, write that down. In the space below, summarize what you learned from the audit.

_____

_____

_____

_____

_____

- For the next two weeks, write and deliver at least three thank-you notes every day to one or two of your constituents. Note the results.

_____

_____

_____

_____

_____

- Find someone in or outside of your organization you think is much better at Encouraging the Heart than you are. Interview that person about what he or she does that enables him or her to engage in this leadership practice. Summarize what you've learned that you can apply to your own situation.

_____

_____

_____

_____

_____

- For the next two weeks, consciously make Encouraging the Heart part of your life at work, at home, in the community, while shopping, while eating out, while participating in an athletic activity. See what it's like to "live with" this practice. After two weeks, note what you did and the results below.

_____

_____

_____

_____

_____

_____

_____

DWYSYWD AUDIT

My Values

What I Do to Live Out These Values

_____   _____

_____   _____

_____   _____

_____   _____

_____   _____

_____   _____

_____   _____

_____   _____

_____   _____

_____   _____

_____   _____

_____   _____

_____   _____

_____   _____

_____   _____

_____   _____

Chapter 10

Moving Forward

Now that I have seen the effects of Encouraging the Heart in action, I understand the profound impacts they have. I will use them more strategically next time and create even stronger bonds and community spirit among team members.

—Melissa Rutledge-Pierce, Maxtor Corporation

The root of the word "encourage" means heart. Leaders understand that, in order to accomplish the extraordinary, people must have strong and committed hearts. When offering encouragement to another person, the leader is in fact providing courage and strength to that person's heart.

There are virtually unlimited ways to show appreciation for accomplishments and to encourage perseverance. Leadership is much more an affair of the heart than merely a matter of the mind. Never underestimate the meaningful and lasting impact your genuine words of encouragement can have on others.

To keep people inspired and willing to persevere on the long and challenging path to success, you need to apply what you've learned about Encouraging the Heart by:

- Making it a point to continually recognize excellence of individuals and teams.

- Providing words of support and encouragement to express your belief and confidence in others.

- Showing your appreciation for both the big and small things your constituents do to achieve goals and model core values.

There are thousands of ways to Encourage the Heart. You've thought about many of them as you've gone through an Encouraging the Heart Workshop or completed the chapters of this workbook on your own. What others can you think of right now? Write at least five ideas below. (Better yet, stretch yourself to ten—you can do it!)

_____

_____

_____

_____

_____

_____

_____

_____

_____

At the back of this workbook you'll find more ideas to help you Encourage the Heart. Keep on collecting them. Write your ideas in a notebook or keep them in a computer file.

DEVELOP AN ACTION PLAN

As a final exercise before you finish this workbook, make a commitment to apply what you've learned about Encouraging the Heart. Write down:

- One action you'll take during the next three weeks to improve your ability to Encourage the Heart

_____

_____

_____

_____

_____

- One action you'll take to recognize and reward one of your constituents who does something to advance the organization's standards

_____

_____

_____

_____

_____

- One action you'll take to recognize and reward *yourself* for achieving those two goals!

_____

_____

_____

_____

_____

_____

Sign your name here: _____

Now, give yourself a standing ovation for having learned and practiced the essential skills for Encouraging the Heart! Your desire to Encourage the Heart is worth celebrating. Thank you, and all best wishes.

IDEAS FOR ENCOURAGING THE HEART

Encouragement comes wrapped in packages of all kinds. We've seen it done in quiet ways with a thank-you, a story, and a smile; and we've been part of grand Academy Awards–style productions.

You already have some ideas from an Encourage the Heart Workshop or the activities in this workbook. Below are some others. (If you'd like more, see our book, *Encouraging the Heart*, pp. 151–175.) We've categorized the ideas under the seven essentials so you can focus your attention on those areas you feel need to be worked on most. But as you'll see, many of these actions include elements of more than one essential.

Most important, have fun with this. Your imagination is the only limit. These activities are designed to facilitate your learning, and learning to do a better job of Encouraging the Heart should be a joyous process.

THE FIRST ESSENTIAL: SET CLEAR STANDARDS

1. Take time to clarify the values or "operating principles" that are important for you and your team to live by. Write down your answer to this question: "What are the values that I believe should guide my daily decisions and actions, and those of the people with whom I work and interact?" We sometimes refer to this as the "credo memo" exercise. It's like a note you might send your colleagues before taking off for an extended sabbatical,

explaining the principles you want them to use to govern their actions and decisions while you're not around. If you've already written down your values, ask yourself, "To what extent do these *still* represent the values I believe should guide our daily decisions and actions? Is there anything I want to add? To delete? Any priorities I want to change?"

2. Ask your associates—those with whom you work regularly—to do the same exercise. Emphasize the areas of agreement and seek consensus around those ideas that are at variance with one another.

3. Post your values statement conspicuously where you know you'll be reminded of your principles regularly. Put a copy in your wallet. Put one in your planner. Put it on your bulletin board. Use it as a screen saver on your computer.

4. Make the topic of one of your next team meetings "Our Values." Ask everyone to state aloud what they believe in. Listen and observe. What are the values that everyone seems to share in common? What values seem to be unique to some individuals? Are there any major values conflicts? Talk about how you can honor individual values and yet as a team have common values that govern your collective behavior. Post collective values in your workplace common areas.

5. If your organization has a corporate creed, or some kind of published statement of values, then set yours, your team's, and the organization's values credos side-by-side. To what extent are they compatible? To what extent are there some conflicts? How good a fit is there between organizational and personal values? What needs to be changed? What needs recommitment?

6. Make sure that people receive regular, specific feedback on their progress toward goals. The feedback can come from you: "Hey, we've reached a project milestone. Well done. Let's celebrate!" Better yet, create ways for people to monitor themselves so they know how much progress they've made.

7. The next time—and every time—you recognize an individual or a group for doing the right thing or doing things right, make sure to announce the standard. Announce it at the beginning, and repeat it at the end. Say something like, "One of the things we stand for around here is knock-your-socks-off service to our customers. Just yesterday, Bev did something to exemplify that value. Let me tell you about it. . . . And remember, just as Bev did, let's knock their socks off every time!"

8. Take a class or read a book on how to set goals and one on how to give performance feedback.

9. Invent or select some symbolic ways of visibly marking people's progress, as the scouts and the military do. Pins, ribbons, badges, patches, medals, certificates, etc., that signify "You made it to the next level" send meaningful messages to the recipients and to their friends, families, and colleagues.

THE SECOND ESSENTIAL: EXPECT THE BEST

1. Assign people to important tasks that aren't part of their defined jobs. Let them know you have assigned them these special jobs because you believe they have the capacity to excel at them. Make a binding commitment to supply the training, resources, authority, and coaching they need to be successful.

2. The ability to create mental images and clearly communicate them to others is a critical leadership skill. Practice envisioning. Picture a sunset at the beach with the waves washing against the shore . . . A gently flowing stream in a cool forest on a hot summer day . . . A meadow of yellow wildflowers in full bloom in springtime . . . A hundred-foot waterfall rushing to a valley floor as the snow melts. Describe these scenes to another person in all their rich color and texture.

   Apply the same visualizing technique to imagine scenes of what you want to accomplish as a leader. Picture yourself and your team reaching the summit of your aspirations, whatever that might currently be. Describe the scene to others in great detail, just as you described the sunset at the beach or the waterfall rushing to the valley floor. Create a richly textured image of your future, and see it, smell it, taste it, hear it, touch it. The better you are at doing this, the more likely your group will be to reach higher levels of performance.

3. Buy some inspirational posters and put them on the walls of your facility. Look for posters with images that symbolize the spirit you'd like to promote in your workplace.

4. When you are coaching or training someone to do something new, tell him or her that you know that this skill is something that can be acquired, and you know he or she can learn it. Even if you think it's obvious, say it out loud anyway.

5. Rent a video or CD of Martin Luther King's "I Have a Dream" speech, delivered at the Lincoln Memorial in Washington, D.C., in 1963. Listen for the word pictures Dr. King paints. Now try to add word pictures to your own speeches.

THE THIRD ESSENTIAL: PAY ATTENTION

1. Don't wait for a ceremony as a reason to recognize someone. As soon as you notice something that deserves immediate recognition, go up to the person and say something like, "I was just noticing how you handled that customer complaint. The way you listened actively and responded was a real model of what we're looking for. What you've done is an example to everyone. Thank you."

2. Carry around coupons for a free beverage at the local coffee or juice shop and give them out when you see people doing something right.

3. Put your key constituents' birthdays and anniversary dates of joining the organization on your calendar. Send a note or drop by for a visit when those special dates come up.

4. Walk in another's shoes for a while. Volunteer to do someone's job. Roll up your shirtsleeves and jump in. People appreciate your efforts, and you gain a better understanding of what your colleagues do.

5. Imagine that you are watching a video of your daily wanderings for the past week. What behavioral signals are you sending? Do they communicate that you're looking for people doing things right and doing the right things? Or do they announce that the sheriff's in town? What specific behaviors can you adopt that communicate, *"I'm here to find all the positive examples that I can?"*

6. Make a list from memory of the objects that each of your key constituents has in her workspace. Then go pay a visit to see how accurate your memory is. Spend time with the people whose workspaces you couldn't recall—in their spaces.
   If you're a virtual company and don't have the opportunity to visit everyone you work with, ask people to describe to you in detail their workspaces. Ask them probing questions about what's on their desks, what's on the walls, etc. Tell them you're trying to get a feel for their spaces in the same way that you do with the people down the hall.

7. For the next lunch hour, hang out at the table with your team, with no agenda. Just get to know each other and talk about whatever's on your minds.

8. At your next team meeting, disclose something about yourself that others don't know, something that enables others to get to know you a little better: the number of brothers and sisters you have, what it was like growing up in your house, your first memory of working in the organization, your favorite screw-up of all time, anything that makes you more open to others. Encourage the others to do the same.

THE FOURTH ESSENTIAL: PERSONALIZE RECOGNITION

1. Tell people in your organization your own "most meaningful recognition story." Ask them to tell theirs. What are the common lessons?

2. The next time you give a speech on behalf of your organization and you have to wear a name tag, wear the name of someone in your organization other than yourself. Notice how it feels to do this. How might it feel to be the other person, knowing that you're wearing his or her name tag?

3. At the end of one of your speeches, say something like, "My colleagues at Challenge, Inc., couldn't be with me today. I sure hope I represented them well."

4. Give your customers, vendors, and employees movie tickets or coupons redeemable for some kind of prize as rewards for doing something exceptional.

5. Make every effort to personalize every recognition event so that the man or woman receiving it feels uniquely appreciated. For the avid bicyclist in your office, for instance, recognize him with a small plastic model of a bike for the desktop; attach a note that says, "For a quick spin around the block when you're working late."

6. Every time you plan an act of recognition, ask yourself, "What can I do to make sure this is special, dramatic, and unique for this person? How can I do the equivalent of putting a part in the freezer or writing a letter addressed to the associate's son?" If you plan to present some kind of gift, ask yourself, "Is this something the individual would appreciate?"

7. Create symbols for certain kinds of recognition in your organization. Choose a logo or symbol. For example, you might choose a zebra. You'll be amazed at how many zebra T-shirts, zebra cups, zebra mugs, zebra pencils, zebra pins, zebra cards, and zebra what-have-you's there are! Be creative devising your rewards; have fun with them.

8. Publish captioned photos or the names of people you want to recognize in a company newsletter, annual report, or department handout. If there's room, include a brief story describing the person's special contribution. Create your organization's Hall of Fame: an area for small plaques, photos, or even handwritten notes, recognizing people who've done extraordinary things.

9. Make a contribution to an employee's favorite charity and announce it at a company party or department get-together.

10. Take a class or workshop on creativity, drawing, painting, or photography. Learn to use a software program for creating exciting graphics. Take a course on advertising and promotion to study words and images that inspire people; translate those methods into Encouraging the Heart.

11. Say thank you personally every time you appreciate something someone does, anywhere and any time. It's good practice and good manners.

THE FIFTH ESSENTIAL: TELL THE STORY

1. The next time you recognize an individual or group, tell the story of what was done in as much detail as you can. If possible, figure out a way to re-enact the incident.

2. Make the only agenda item for one of your team meetings that each person—including you—tells the story of his or her most meaningful recognition.

3. Make the only agenda item of another team meeting the telling of stories on the theme of "I heard something good about you," about someone else on the team they work with.

4. Don't wait for meetings or special events to tell stories about how people in the organization have gone above and beyond the call of duty. Hallways, elevators, cafeterias, voice mail, and e-mail are all acceptable venues for telling brief stories.

5. Keep a journal. Record in as much detail as you can the critical incidents of each day. Capture as many examples of outstanding and commendable performance as you can. The practice of observing and recording is important in building your skills in storytelling.

6. Incorporate storytelling into your next strategic planning process. Pledge that you will no longer accept bulleted points on overheads as an acceptable plan for the future.

7. Ask a professional storyteller to participate in one of your leadership seminars and share tips on good storytelling. Or take a class in storytelling

8. At the next holiday when you're together with your family or friends, volunteer to read a story fit for the occasion.

9. At dinner every night, don't just talk about the day; tell a story about it. Describe the rich details of place, people, and feelings. Use your home as a practice stage.

10. Attend a reading at a local bookstore featuring a fiction writer you like. Listen to how he or she reads stories.

11. Interview an actor who does improvisational theater. Ask him or her to share some ways of taking a simple idea and turning it into a story.

THE SIXTH ESSENTIAL: CELEBRATE TOGETHER

1. When planning a celebration, ask yourself about the fundamental principles that are being honored as well as how you're gong to have fun.

2. Visit a party store for ideas on how to make celebrations more festive. Always keep a few party favors handy. You never know when you might want to throw a spontaneous celebration should an employee announce a wedding, a birth, or other personal achievement.

3. Visit an organization that has a reputation for being a fun place to work. Find out what makes them so inventive when it comes to celebration.

4. When you attend high school and college athletic events, watch the cheerleaders, coaches, and players as they celebrate small and large victories. Focus on their

enthusiasm and energy. Watch how the people expressing this enthusiasm and those who receive it are affected. Notice how *you* are affected by the celebrations.

5. At a wedding or other celebratory event, make mental notes on what you like or on what really inspires you about the event. See whether you can incorporate some of these ideas into your plans for Encouraging the Heart.

6. If your organization doesn't do much celebrating, start an informal celebration task force. Make it your job to liven up the place, borrowing where you can from the inventiveness of others and creating your own fun and games at work. Plan festive celebrations for even the smaller milestones that your team reaches. Immediate acknowledgment keeps energy and enthusiasm high.

7. Organize informal ways to bring people together: special lunches, picnics, noontime athletic events (volleyball, shooting baskets, softball game, etc.), anything that promotes camaraderie and interpersonal support. Put a microwave in the vicinity of your office door. Every afternoon, make some popcorn and invite folks to take a break and join you for a brief discussion about how the day is going. If popcorn isn't your thing, how about an ice cream vending machine, a jar of candies, or a basket of fruit?

8. Put up a "bragging board" in your workspace. Post notes of appreciation from customers, vendors, and colleagues. Invite everyone to contribute notes and pictures of themselves and others.

9. Mark particularly significant transitions with special celebrations—things like company anniversaries, a merger or acquisition, the launch of a new product, etc. Ask yourself what you can do to make the event unique and memorable. When organizing the celebration—any celebration—make sure everyone knows when and where it is and what it's about.

10. Involve other people in planning celebrations. Don't try to do it all yourself. Joint planning offers social support, gets people to laugh together, and generates more creativity than if one person handles everything.

11. Visit your local comedy club or take classes to learn to laugh and joke around.

THE SEVENTH ESSENTIAL: SET THE EXAMPLE

1. Get personally involved in as many recognition events and celebrations as possible. If you don't attend staff celebrations, you're sending the message that you're not interested. That lack of interest is sure to be mirrored back to you.

2. Identify those experiences in your life that truly inspire you, and bring this kind of inspiration into your conversations with employees.

3. Ask a colleague to give you feedback on how well you are Encouraging the Heart. Ask him or her for suggestions on how to improve.

4. Every time you start a meeting, affirm your personal commitment to the values that you all share. There's something about frequent repetition of a commitment that starts you moving in that direction. The more people you tell and the more often you say it, the harder it is to back out.

5. Identify a positive role model for each of the seven essentials of Encouraging the Heart. Make sure you can envision in your mind someone who does each of these practices well.

6. Create your own recognition reminder notice, screen saver, or other device for making visible the ways in which you can Encourage the Heart.

7. Make sure that others know about your efforts to model encouragement. Tell people stories about how you tried and succeeded, or tried and failed. Share the lessons you've learned.

8. Keep a journal of your experiments with Encouraging the Heart. What works for you? What doesn't? What lessons have you learned? How has this effort changed you as a leader?

9. The next time someone recognizes you, make note of your own thoughts and feelings. (Experience becomes the best teacher, but only if we reflect on it.) Then send that person a thank-you note expressing appreciation for what you learned.

10. Offer to teach a course on Encouraging the Heart. The best way to learn something is to teach it to someone else. You certainly remember how much more you prepared for something when you actually had to be the one in front of the classroom.

Notes

CHAPTER 2. THE SEVEN ESSENTIALS OF ENCOURAGING THE HEART

1. Kepner-Tregoe, *People and Their Jobs: What's Real, What's Rhetoric?* Princeton, NJ: Kepner-Tregoe, 1995, p. 5.
2. Telephone interview with Jodi Taylor, vice president, Center for Creative Leadership, Colorado Springs, Colorado, April 1998.
3. I. Federman, remarks to the Leavey School of Business, Santa Clara University, April 2, 1991.
4. Graham, G. H. "Going the Extra Mile: Motivating Your Workers Doesn't Always Involve Money." *San Jose Mercury News,* January 7, 1987, p. 4C.
5. R. M. Kanter, in presentation at Santa Clara University on "The Change Masters," March 13, 1986.
6. Melohn, T. *The New Partnership: Profit by Bringing Out the Best in Your People, Customers, and Yourself.* Essex Junction, VT: Oliver Wright, 1994, p. 225.

CHAPTER 3. SET CLEAR STANDARDS

7. Eden, D. *Pygmalion in Management: Productivity as a Self-Fulfilling Prophecy.* Lexington, MA: Lexington Books, 1990.
8. Bandura, A., & Cervone, D. "Self-Evaluation and Self-Efficacy Mechanisms Governing the Motivational Effects of Goal Systems." *Journal of Personality and Social Psychology,* 1983, *45,* 1017.

CHAPTER 4. EXPECT THE BEST

9. Manzoni, J. F., & Barsoux, J. L. "The Set-Up-to-Fail Syndrome." *Harvard Business Review,* March-April 1998, pp. 101–113.

CHAPTER 5. PAY ATTENTION

10. Boyer, G. "Turning Points in the Development of Male Servant-Leaders." (Ph.D. dissertation, Fielding Institute, 1997.)
11. Fisher, R., & Brown, S. *Getting Together.* Boston: Houghton Mifflin, 1988.

12. Ross, J. A. "Does Friendship Improve Job Performance?" *Harvard Business Review,* March-April 1997, pp. 8–9. See also Jehn, K.A., and Shah, P.P., "Interpersonal Relationships and Task Performance: An Examination of Medicating Processes in Friendship and Acquaintance Groups." *Journal of Personality and Social Psychology,* 1997, *72*(4), 775–790.

CHAPTER 7. TELL THE STORY

13. Martin, J., & Powers, M. "Organizational Stories: More Vivid and Persuasive Than Quantitative Data." In B. W. Shaw (Ed.), *Psychological Foundations of Organizational Behavior* (2nd ed.). Glenview, IL: Scott, Foresman, 1983.
14. Wilkens, A. L. "Organizational Stories as Symbols Which Control the Organization." In L. R. Pondy and others (Eds.), *Organizational Symbolism.* Greenwhich, CT: JAI Press, 1983. See also D. Armstrong, *Managing by Storying Around: A New Method of Leadership.* New York: Doubleday Currency, 1992.
15. For more information on this study and other story research, see G. Shaw, R. Brown, and P. Bromiley, "Strategic Stories: How 3M Is Rewriting Business Planning." *Harvard Business Review,* May-June 1998, pp. 41–50.
16. Gardner, H. *Leading Minds.* New York: Basic Books, 1995, p. 43.
17. Klein, G. *The Sources of Power: How People Make Decisions.* Cambridge, MA: MIT Press, 1998, pp. 177–178.

CHAPTER 8. CELEBRATE TOGETHER

18. DeForest, C. "The Art of Celebration: A New Concept for Today's Leaders." In J. D. Adams (Ed.), *Transforming Leadership from Vision to Results.* Alexandria, VA: Miles River Press, 1986, p. 223.

Acknowledgments

This new edition of *The Encouraging the Heart Workbook* is a testimony to the fact that writing and publishing are highly collaborative efforts. It takes a community of committed and passionate professionals to go from idea to bound book, and every time we engage in a writing project we are reminded of the enduring truth that you can't do it alone.

Lisa Shannon, associate publisher at Wiley, has been the driving force behind making our work more accessible and more practical, and she was the original champion for the *Encouraging the Heart Workbook*. Lisa demonstrates daily what it means to reward and recognize others, and while she is not a case in our books, she ought to be. The acquiring editor for this workbook was Marisa Kelley. Marisa gracefully and masterfully coordinated the team that brought this book to print. Without Marisa, we wouldn't have these pages to share with our readers.

Janis Chan, an accomplished writer and instructional designer, had the task of crafting the first edition of this workbook. We've worked with Janis before on *The Leadership Challenge Workbook*, and she has immense talent for knowing just the right question to ask or activity to try in order to put principles into practice. For this new edition of *The Encouraging the Heart Workbook*, we turned to Leslie Stephen, our trusted developmental editor for the fourth edition of *The Leadership Challenge*. With great skill and artistry she helped us craft this revision of the original, as well as working to create the *Facilitator's Guide* that accompanies it. Leslie has a gift for bringing our material to life in story, example, and practical activities. She's also disciplined about details and schedules, and we are grateful that she was able to collaborate with us on this project.

The production crew for this edition included Dawn Kilgore and Rebecca Taff at Wiley. They turned text into a printed book. If it weren't for their extraordinary talent, the manuscript would be collecting dust. Book production takes persistence, creativity, artistry, attention to detail, professionalism, patience, and much more. We continue to marvel at the skill every time we see a finished book on the shelves.

The most rewarding part of writing a book, of course, is knowing that our readers find it of value. Our thanks to all of you who strive to improve your families, your communities, and your workplaces. Your leadership is making a difference.

First, last, and always, we thank our families for their unending support for the work we've chosen. They are the ones who encourage our hearts daily, and we are extremely fortunate to be so blessed. We offer a special thanks to Jackie Schmidt-Posner and Tae Kouzes, who make all this worthwhile.

About the Authors

Jim Kouzes and Barry Posner are co-authors of the award-winning and best-selling book, *The Leadership Challenge*. This book was selected as one of the top ten books on leadership of all time (according to *The 100 Best Business Books of All Time*), won the James A. Hamilton Hospital Administrators' Book-of-the-Year Award, won the Critics' Choice Award from the nation's book review editors, was a *BusinessWeek* best-seller, and has sold over 1.8 million copies in more than twenty languages. Jim and Barry have co-authored more than a dozen other leadership books, including *A Leader's Legacy*—selected by *Soundview Executive Book Summaries* as one of the top thirty books of the year—*Credibility*: *How Leaders Gain It and Lose It, Why People Demand It*—chosen by *Industry Week* as one of its year's five best management books—*Encouraging the Heart*, *The Student Leadership Challenge*, and *The Academic Administrator's Guide to Exemplary Leadership*. They also developed the highly acclaimed *Leadership Practices Inventory* (LPI), a 360-degree questionnaire for assessing leadership behavior, which is one of the most widely used leadership assessment instruments in the world. More than four hundred doctoral dissertations and academic research projects have been based on The Five Practices of Exemplary Leadership® model.

Among the honors and awards that Jim and Barry have received are the American Society for Training and Development's (ASTD) highest award for Distinguished Contribution to Workplace Learning and Performance; Management/Leadership Educators of the Year by the International Management Council (this honor puts them in the company of Ken Blanchard, Stephen Covey, Peter Drucker, Edward Deming, Frances Hesselbein, Lee Iacocca, Rosabeth Moss Kanter, Norman Vincent Peale, and Tom Peters, who are all past recipients of the award); and named among the top fifty leadership coaches in the nation (according to *Coaching for Leadership*).

Jim and Barry are frequent conference speakers, and each has conducted leadership development programs for hundreds of organizations, including Apple, Applied Materials, ARCO, AT&T, Australia Post, Bank of America, Bose, Charles Schwab, Cisco Systems, Community Leadership Association, Conference Board of Canada, Consumers Energy, Dell Computer, Deloitte Touche, Dorothy Wylie Nursing Leadership Institute, Egon Zehnder International, Federal Express, Gymboree, Hewlett-Packard, IBM, Jobs DRSingapore, Johnson & Johnson, Kaiser Foundation Health Plans and Hospitals, L.L. Bean, Lawrence Livermore National Labs, Lucile Packard Children's Hospital, Merck, Mervyn's, Motorola, NetApp, Northrop Grumman, Roche Bioscience, Siemens, Standard Aero, Sun Microsystems, 3M, Toyota, the U.S. Postal Service, United Way, USAA, Verizon, VISA, and The Walt Disney Company.

James M. Kouzes is the Dean's Executive Professor of Leadership, Leavey School of Business, at Santa Clara University. Not only is he a highly regarded leadership scholar and an experienced executive, but *The Wall Street Journal* has cited him as one of the twelve best executive educators in the United States. In 2006 Jim was presented with the Golden Gavel, the highest honor awarded by Toastmasters International. Jim served as president, CEO, and chairman of the Tom Peters Company from 1988 through 1999, and prior to that led the Executive Development Center at Santa Clara University (1981 to 1987). Jim founded the Joint Center for Human Services Development at San Jose State University (1972 to 1980) and was on the staff of the School of Social Work, University of Texas. His career in training and development began in 1969 when he conducted seminars for Community Action Agency staff and volunteers in the war on poverty effort. Following graduation from Michigan State University (B.A. with honors in political science), he served as a Peace Corps volunteer (1967–1969). Jim also received a certificate from San Jose State University's School of Business for completion of the internship in organization development. Jim can be reached at jim@kouzes.com.

Barry Z. Posner is a professor of leadership at Santa Clara University (Silicon Valley, California), where he has received numerous teaching and innovation awards and served as dean of the Leavey School of Business for twelve years (1996 to 2009). An internationally renowned scholar and educator, Barry is author or co-author of more than a hundred research and practitioner-focused articles. He currently serves on the editorial review boards for *Leadership and Organizational Development, Leadership Review,* and *The International Journal of Servant-Leadership*. Barry is a warm and engaging conference speaker and dynamic workshop facilitator. Barry received his baccalaureate degree with honors from the University of California, Santa Barbara, in political science; his master's degree from The Ohio State University in public administration; and his doctoral degree from the University of Massachusetts, Amherst, in organizational behavior and administrative theory. Having consulted with a wide variety of public- and private-sector organizations around the globe, Barry currently sits on the board of directors of EMQ Family First. He served previously on the board of the American Institute of Architects (AIA), Junior Achievement of Silicon Valley and Monterey Bay, San Jose Repertory Theater, Public Allies, Big Brothers/Big Sisters of Santa Clara County, the Center for Excellence in Nonprofits, Sigma Phi Epsilon Fraternity, and several start-up companies. Barry can be reached at bposner@scu.edu.

Notes

Notes

Notes

Notes

Notes

Notes

Notes

Notes

Notes